ampersonate

ampersonate

Tyler Friend

choose the sword press * 2014
ctspress.com

Acknowledgements:

"Fresh Flesh" was previously published in decomP magazinE.

"I wrote it. It must be true." and "Falling in Love with Semi-Fictional
Characters" were previously published in Saint Vincent College's Generation
Magazine.

Contents

Falling in Love with Semi-Fictional Characters

She formed her skin from Starbucks cups,
her wings from torn tights.
Her cheeks
were freckled with dewberries.
Her veins,
filled with chlorophyll.

Perched on the blanket border,
she sang me lullabies
and ate my molded cheeses.

Overhead, bats overcast the sky,
pulling in the cloud covers.

Behind the band shell:
black-eyed Susans
and blue-eyed boys
(blowing bubbles,
dangling dragonflies).

Listen to the cushion plants percolate.
Receive parcels of air.

Do things just for their symbolic resonance.

Reclaim corks:
soak them in spirits,
release them like fireflies.
Curtsy to female ivy.
Find a way to distill the moonlight.

Suck the honey from her lips.
Rename her Honeysuckle in your head.

I wrote it. It must be true

First, I vomited in the garbage can
(that may have been an armchair)
and wiped my nose on film overexposed.

I saw aquariums brewing illusions.
The bartend said, "That one's yours. They're steeped exclusive."
I saw overripe apricots,
amber and amethyst,
black widow webs,
empty pills, and a pearlescent paintbrush.

May also contain:
tobacco mosaic, beet yellow, brackish brine, bristlecone pine.

Instructions:
Ingest entire batch.
Record everything: you won't remember.
Stay with your batch buddy.
Live by the mantra, *I wrote it. It must be true.*

"Whither wander you?"

The serotinal air shivers. Whitings wither.
Kudzu clambers up cambering elm, invading floral realm.
Fairy ring and misfit stream.
Blanket bog, blue sun fog,
bed rough, honey tuft.

Take selfies with fairies: Moth, Mustardseed, and Cicada.
Share their aphid honey and beebread.
Your hands fumble, fancy-sick. Eyelashes mumble.

Hair moss pillows under the willow.
Remix circadian rhythms
with the changing of the seasons.

"I'll eat you like an apricot."
"No. Explore me like a spelunker."

The Female Woodcutter's Aria

She led me into the stretched tissue time of still wet webs, away from the diesel breath drag. Figures sat amongst ferns and bushes and bloomers. Beings of dreamtime whispered into existence. The sweet smell of bound periodicals saturated the air. Lovers wrestled (malaria-like), bitten by bookworms.

The rainwater perfume was a bargain, but I asked if I could trade some of my hair instead. She said she would prefer skin. I said I was offended, and she thought it was because she called me "Sir."

The shuffling morticians ate circles of music, communed with specters, and sought corpses to adore. Oh, the face. The center of percussion: the cringes, the bras, and the crystal.

Triple X is fine, but intersex isn't even defined. Read between the lines. Chrome your zones. The queen said, "Honey, you don't need to respect your elders, but you do need to respect anyone in a wheelchair. Really."

We found hogs suckling cynicisms and smog. We found blogs that didn't post soft grunge or soft porn. We snorted in as much dust as we could and ate all of the dandelions.

The cannon of liquor melted the perfume off of her face. Her fishnets were like rural roads paved with mist. I poured her the seventh ornamental vintage and she ate the impossible parties. Her precious influence maintained a passive brightness. She confided with incandescent innocence:

Come Dream with Us

Act I

Food trucks park outside the Parthenon,
next to the knit-clad tree,
serving Cheerwine floats, mint-soaked watermelon,
pork barbeque with brie.

Act II

How far did you travel to be here tonight?
Program, stickers, survey,
check all that apply:
Nashville native, college student, gay/lesbian/trans/bi.

Act III

A homemade t-shirt reading,
Puck my Life.
A man with pink hair
feeding grapes to his wife.

Act IV

The way you wear the sea
in your glasses.
The way your lips
are just a little too red.

Act V

C'mon, you hopeful monsters,
allow the world to grow around you.

A Midnight in Summer

I think he might have loved me
like violence in a field of daisies
or children playing at romance.

So much light and so much dark:
mysterious deaths and cigarettes.

Lined eyes, sundresses:
questionably marked cheeks.

Holding daffodils
in a conversation with old ministers.

Little summers smoking,
asking if I knew the boy who died.

Football in the garden,
benches turned to headstones.

Sam catches better than any of the boys.
Caroline and Sam look the same.

Wanting—comfort—condolences:
linen lingerie.

On stage: crying, backstage: trying to explain
his camera equipment.

Printing animations: only the people
are gray: a world in high contrast.

It's time to compose symphonies aloud.

Lullaby Lectures

A hopeless contagion wracked his body,
a momentary capturing of being:
vision(ary): mimesis (is boring).

Poppies, ticks:
playmates, small friends, toys.
Kudzu: playful stuff.

Shoes soaked with hard water:
the innocence of ants.

Absinthe ekphrasis,
a condensing, a collage.

Ambrosia: food of the gods.
Abrosia: a lack of food.

            Cajun tears, his father's beet farm.

Pre-mammary, embryonic
(amber tonic, strange sighs):
the richest alchemy.

Knotty oaks: naughty tokes.
Piano lullaby lectures: Olivier sway.

Vespers, Whispers

Bas(e) i lica bitch faces
ass emble in the dungeon.
Snape stands in the corner,
her hair slick and her smirk tang

ible. Lots of white kids in black robes:
high heels and high tops,
crisp s lack s and paint-caked jeans.

                              Poetry in my pants,
                              art up her sleeve,
                              and a flask in my back pocket
                              (just in case).

Cacophonous homi-
lies, beaming bi-
shops, and choir girls
so pretty
I n early

puke.

Ext.

I tried
to paint her as she was before:

skin pale
sanguine,
concrete outlines around
eyes rusting blue,
shadows veined with scars.

She was a syringe full of water.

Fresh Flesh

Blood-let.
Honey / cut.

Undercover smut:
long-overdue books
(plaque ghosts).

Im polite hosts,
overcast eyelashes,
and un(der)paid maids.

In order to pro-
duce us, our mother had to l-
earn the trick of budding.

Cact us ju ice t rip.

It's a world that's alive.

Armed with their own gods,
they bind brains,
form skulls to fit,
and trepan out any inconsistencies.

Lilith

(the little lesbian
demon who lives
inside me)
took control for the night.

She bought me a bra
and turned a scarf into a skirt.

I ended up on a couch with
an evil queen,
the Cheshire cat,
an obscure black character,
and a hippie couple
(although I don't think they were in costume).

A short Danny Zuko asked me what I was.
I squeezed my boobs in reply.
"Swag!"
We bro-hugged
(a feat I've yet to accomplish while male).
Sandy either checked me out or eyed me suspiciously.

The queen let me drink all of her wine.
The guy with the bandana shared his electronic cigarette.

My skirt is still there.

Home from the Office

Last night, I dreamt my wife
texted me, *Be at the stove
when I get home.*

I put on an apron and took off everything else.

I dreamt thigh-
highs and mushrooms,
eyeliner and he(i)r-

(b)looms, bras and broilers.
I dreamt me onto my knees,
strap-on mid-mouth and hands
on hips, in hair, between my br-
easts: unknown lands.

Germaphobe Romance

I first realized
the extent of my love
when I didn't feel
a compulsion to
sanitize my hands
after they were in-
side you.

Manic Pixie Drummer Girl

Tyler told me that he was in love
with the girl   but was only in love
with the fox sweater.

yea she was a precious bowl of honey nut cheerios

I said I was in love
with the little drummer girl;
I knew   I was only in love with
the possibilities.

omg she's a lesbian good luck

I stand transfixed
by the trajectories of your flailing arms
and the precision you display.

Lead me
through a tunnel
folded from pages of plaster
(which couldn't be left blank)
into a hollow
hazy within exhalations
from unsure lips
and scorched nostrils.

Lines
of light
draw themselves
toward the question marks

punk
too
ate
ing
your eyes.

I watched him watch you
through the lens of his Canon
until you started singing
about my hometown.
You caught my eye,
but you were out of focus.

Contract

So cross your eyes
and I'll spot your *me*.
We'll stay here and contr-
act caring, dis-
own our own in securi ties.

On Hormones and Social Anxiety

A slow, constant trick-
le: fruit f lies, lovers (?)

on rent(, r)ed bicycles:
sexicles. As in, *You are so sexy—*
like a popsicle. As in, *Your boobs look*
like they're about to pop (!)
right outa that bra.

Trucker hat, side-cut:
non-monogamous (queer?),
pencil tucked behind ear.

Stick-and-poke, tattooed arm-
pits: a plastic knife and a used
Band-Aid: cicadas.

As in, *I would never really even try to start a conversation with y'all because*
        I wouldn't want to force even my presence upon you.

But I still want to tell them, *You look like a semicolon.*

10 Steps to Transform Yourself

01. Become a Marilyn Monroe
with armpit hair and hips
formed from sweatpants.

02. Bring on
the on-sale wine
and reservation cigarettes.

03. Use an X-Acto knife to
cut limes in two.

04. Mix lime juice, wine, tequila, and simple syrup.
Sprinkle tears onto the glass's lip.

05. Freeze overnight.

06. Shadow your eyes so they think
you've never seen the sun.
Strap on size 13 heels,
purposefully torn tights,
and a borrowed dress.

07. Encircle your imperfections with green ink.
Get shown all the correct hand positions.
Hope she doesn't ask about the dick you don't always want.

08. When she asks you why,
say it's because she has you
so
fucking
terrified
of getting her pregnant.

09. Ask her why and she'll say it's because
she has to get closer to God.

10. Use an X-Acto knife
to cut two lines in thighs.

cripp/led

black sheet supported by feet
like blanket fort retreat
like please
like why did Daddy leave?

like noisy submarines
and asbestos of the brain
like hollowed out trench veins
tap water dry rot

clothespin creep
Benadryl beat

like how cold always rhymes with bold

like coffee stains and melting planes
like how could you?

like diamond-cut thighs
and girls with boyfriends
and other things that really
shouldn't even matter

Tonight,

I am painting my thighs turquoise.

I am squeezing them closed.

I am holding my arms to my sides.

I am accepting any offer.

I am folding into it.

I am stenciling *be here* onto stained glass.

Hert

This is a rewrite of a rewrite of a rewrite of H.D.'s "Heat."

The wind lends me heat:
tatters me. Fruit drops.

Thighs thicket.
She presses pears:
blunts.

Rain blotches. She
showed me visions of de-
capitated pigeons,
peered through grass.

She cut it, turned it in-
to a path.

The Printed Girl

She's crimson thighs and cyan sighs
and nothing purple at all.

She's hard lines
and slow curves.

She's iron armature bones
and chewed paper flesh.

She's 130 lbs, cold pressed,
and perfect bound.

She's water based, permanent,
and writes on most surfaces.

Avoid eye and skin contact.

Notes to No One

I write notes to no one
and watch the tension
keep them afloat
until they turn gray
and their corners sub
merge.
If I'm careful,
they can stay legible
until I become afraid.

Sometimes I hope
the paper will disintegrate first,
leaving the ink alone
(just for a second)
amidst the ripples
until it joins
forgotten words.

Sometimes I hope
the lake will freeze
while they are still floating
and encase them in
diamond
shard
sheets
until I find someone
to show all the hands
I've held out.

un/tilted

origami notes at Mellow:
an abundance of Katherine's thoughts.

coffee: coughing,
covering up, shaking
from laughter.

candy cigarettes and
Woodchuck (granny smith).

outside McCreary's:
the coolest of kids: Guinness,
strong cigars.

spiders, scars, and
(imagined) turquoise bras.

(peeing behind bushes)

Carousel turnt,
marshmallow hurt,
cotton candy cussing:

jealous joy rides,
circles of pink,
and blue-bag—barf

(recyclables). Corn dog cart-
ridge: primed and ready.
Ketchup-syrup sick,

Moldy Peaches melody
(in the background): coughs
and cookie dough.

The Caterpillar and The Whip:
ridden in quick succession until cheap
circus freak squeaks:

nauseous knees and elbow-bent
dreams unhook every button
of each balloon scheme.

Memoration

This darkroom was full
of sentences, and we were
trying to become
a paragraph, filling ourselves with orange p
unch, discussions of gender politics, Nietzsche,
and female mastur bation:
typewriter trash talk.

Our hands printed the walls red.
We knotted philosophy in
to balloon-shaped animals.

He said, *He's like Confucius with a baseball cap and a flannel.*

I said, *He represents an engrained patriarchy of peeing in the sink.*

Window habitats coexisted
    out of habit.
We knit to
    get her consonants and crocheted
clandestine moments in
to something completely tangible.

We need a new sentence, one that has never been developed before.

We dreamt our space into
existence, outlined
clouds for clarity,
brushed pining off
shagged carpet.

Laughs flashed before
my closed eyes.

Close the window;
        the wind is
blow ing a way all
o f o ur syll ables.

* * *

I was shrouded in shrugs, in
decision, and guilt armor
formed from years
of self-hate and
too many morals.

I took my insecurities out for a picnic,
wrapped up two sandwiches and *Lunch Poems,*
poured a wine float, walked out past the graveyard.

I took off
my shirt (
I thought he might've liked that
) and let the sun mass
age my back.

* * *

He said, *There's a goalie in soccer too, but that doesn't mean you can't score.*

I told him I didn't think
th at t hat
was an appropriate comparison.

He cheated on h
er right before

he wrote h
er that love poem. O
   nly she noticed: h
e said *loved.*

She said, *He dropped a class so that we could have sex.*

She said, *You can't be
contained.* I ran i
t between my teeth
before I complied.

We drug
out each word for
as long as
we could; we
serrated each serif.

The technique wasn't there, but the enthusiasm was amazing.

We used tampons for periods
and livers for semicolons, thought we were
being metaphorically resonant.

We did away with exclamation marks.

We took our pale,
bleached the paper with it.

* * *

I crossed my legs, dotted each of her e
yes. She kissed my ear for so long that s
he ate my eardrum, dreamt
that I married her girlfriend.

Proofreading (reading proves) i
s androgynou
sly symbolic.

She had 14 creases in her forehead, o
r maybe 14 stretch marks on each thigh,
starting to freckle. She was
a sonnet, irregularly pro port ioned.

She formed her smiles from chewed poems,
her hips from creased paper.
The coffee (black)
beneath her freckles
and the whiskey
(honey) in her hip
s caused contusion
s in my chest.

She looked personated.

She said, *I'm not real, so it's okay if I take all my clothes off.*

I was hid den in a tracin
g paper trance, a
con fused run-around dance. The hair t
raced her clavicle and the corres pond ing
synapses in my brain fired off
ovarian fancies, faded into a breath
less iridescence.

I said, *Ask whether he was elected president of the meteorology club.*

He told me, *You'd probably actually make a better girlfriend than her.*

* * *

He was closeted, toasting
time bombs. He was so skinny th
at shoulder joints were rec tangles.

He lit his hair on fire just for fun,
drank creamer straight.
He conducted mi graines
symphonic: poisons, little
whispers, dandy lions.

His foot part enjambed her ribcage.
Her veins pulsed with iron chunks.
The tequila poured from her eyes.

He told me,
You should write poems about me, but
he wouldn't give me anything
to write about, except for the half-shot
of Bakon. I wrote paper lantern love letters.

I said, *I don't like the taste of bananas,*
but I really like eating bananas.
I was infat u ate d.

* * *

She was entranced by the concept of dew,
and was only slightly disappointed when it didn't actually exi
st. She jumped off the roof, fell almost as hard as I did,
hurt her an
kle.

The violin bowed, waxed, waned out
rageously. The tree branche
s sounded like mice.

They smelled like fireflies and fog.

She dreamt us
into the newe
st Stephen King novel.

He coveted my hair; she caressed my scalp excessively.

We welded together
our strongest fears and we check-marked all
the comb
in   ed
obstacles we over
                          came.
We ate the biggest of bit es.

She said, *Can you please give me the remaining alcohol, your mouth?*

We smeared the pun
ctuation onto our lips
and waited
for someone to come correct it.

She had sleepy eyes,
tired thighs, and blood-
speckled panties: an
awkward omission.

I am not very popular, but I am bleeding.

* * *

Overwriting: distractive sounds.
We formed ourselves into different patterns.

They slipped into this chapter,
as if by accident. She was a waterfall
of adjectives. He was a noun
with 11 elongated, distinct definitions.

www.ingramcontent.com/pod-product-compliance
Lightning Source LLC
Chambersburg PA
CBHW071800020426
42331CB00008B/2341